HOLY HUMOR

LIFT YOUR SPIRITS

Publications International, Ltd.

Front Cover: Anne O'Connor

Back Cover: Jonny Hawkins

Contributing Author: When not sitting in church praying for inspiration and taking notes for holy humor books, Paul Seaburn is the head writer for *12th Street Jump*, a jazz-blues-and-comedy show on public radio and writes scripts for many Internet comedy video providers. Check out his latest musings on Facebook.

Cartoonist: Jonny Hawkins, the son of a former pastor and his pianist wife, began drawing cartoons in church while his dad was preaching. In Bible college in 1986, he sold his first to a Sunday School newsletter ... and has been selling them ever since. His work has appeared in *Reader's Digest*, *National Catholic Register*, *Guideposts*, *Parade*, *Focus on the Family*, *Woman's World*, in 77 *Chicken Soup for the Soul* titles and in over 600 other publications. He lives with his wife, Carissa, and their three children near his boyhood home in Sherwood, MI.

Additional Illustrations: Art Explosion, iCLIPART, Jupiterimages, Shutterstock.com

Louis Weber, CEO
Publications International, Ltd.
7373 North Cicero Avenue
Lincolnwood, Illinois 60712

Permission is never granted for commercial purposes.

ISBN-13: 978-1-4508-7824-1
ISBN-10: 1-4508-7824-5

Manufactured in U.S.A.

8 7 6 5 4 3 2 1

Read on and let these quips, stories, cartoons, and jokes lift your spirits to heaven!

Dear Pastor,

My mother is very religious. She goes to play bingo at the church every week even if she has a cold.

Annette, age 8

Dear God,

You don't have to worry about me. I always look both ways.

Melanie, age 7

Dear God,

My brothers told me about being born, but it doesn't sound right. They are just kidding, aren't they?

Marsha, age 9

Dear God,

Who draws the lines around the countries?

Nan, age 9

A minister was flying to California to visit his family when the plane hit some bad turbulence. Passengers bounced up and down, drinks went flying, and babies and adults alike were crying. The pilot came on the intercom briefly to warn them that it would last for a while.

A flight attendant who knew the minister crawled across the floor hanging onto the seats, looked up at him, and begged, "Reverend, everyone is already praying to be saved. Is there something else you can do?"

The minister thought for a moment, then reached into the seat pocket, removed the barf bag, opened it slowly, and took up a collection.

Deacon Don always knew how to raise money. While sitting in a dunking booth at the church picnic, he doubled his contributions just by wearing a sign that said "Goliath."

"Many thanks to the members who donated lightbulbs for the new church offices," the minister said to the congregation. "And now let us sing: 'I Saw the Light.'"

Dear God,

Did you mean for the giraffe to look like that, or was it an accident?

Norma, age 7

"I know what a beatitude is," said Eva. "It's what makes bees buzz."

Bulletin Bloopers

Wednesday at 5:00 PM there will be a meeting of the Little Mothers Club. All wishing to become Little Mothers, please see the minister in his study.

Will all of those with rolls in the church Christmas play please report to the kitchen after the service.

We're looking for volunteers for our prison ministry. You can help put the "con" in "congregation."

***

The rosebud on the altar this morning is to announce the birth of David Alan Balser, the sin of Rev. and Mrs. Julius Balser.

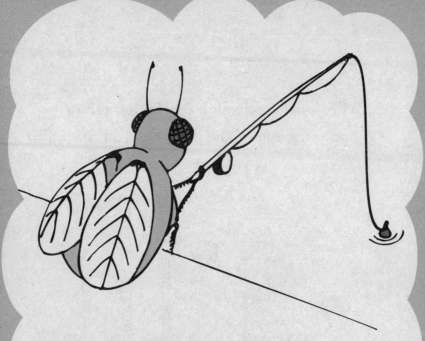

Billy and Bobby's dad decided they were old enough to try fly fishing, so they spent a Saturday afternoon tying flies. Billy was fascinated by the process and said, "I wonder who invented fly fishing."

"That's easy," said Bobby. "It was Noah. How else could he feed all those animals on the boat without using the two worms?"

Dear God,

Of all the people who worked for you,
I like Noah and David best.

Rob, age 7

**"God should have asked Michael
to save the animals,"** Darryl told
his mom, "because he's an ark angel."

"I TRY TO KEEP ALL TEN
COMMANDMENTS, REVEREND, BUT
THERE ARE ONLY SEVEN DAYS IN
THE WEEK!"

Mike and Matt were arguing about the Ten Commandments. Mike said, "God put the Ten Commandments on stone instead of paper so they would last forever."

"That's not it," replied Matt. "God put the Ten Commandments on stone instead of paper so we wouldn't cut them up and rearrange them by preference."

***

Reverend Martha came up with a list of no-nos for the church camping trip. She called them her Tent Commandments.

A man walked up to the counter at a religious store and took out his wallet while handing the clerk a bumper sticker that read, "WWJD?"

"What does this stand for?" he asked.

"What would Jesus do?" replied the clerk.

The man looked at the bumper sticker and then handed it back to the clerk as he put his wallet back in his pocket. "Is there something wrong with it?" she asked him.

"No," said the man. "I just figured that Jesus would have walked."

Mark explained to his parents, "Jesus used to fly on an airplane, and Pontius was the pilot!"

While grading his term papers, a college professor noticed something familiar about all of the papers except for one and realized he had uncovered a major cheating scandal. As he handed back each paper marked with a big red F, he told the students it was because they had received help writing the papers instead of doing them on their own.

When he reached the last student, he asked him to stand up and told the class that this was the only person who did not receive any help. The student looked at him sheepishly and said, "I received help from God."

The professor said, "No you didn't," and handed him a paper marked with a big red F.

On the first day of class, the English professor asked her students what kind of writers they wanted to be. "I want to be like Jesus," one girl answered.

Not knowing what she meant, the professor asked the girl to explain.

"My brother took this class last semester," she said. "He worked all night on his final paper and it was brilliant. Right before he printed it, the power went out, his computer went down, and he lost everything and flunked this class. That's why I want to be a writer like Jesus. Jesus saves."

"This homework is too much for dial-a-prayer," Ellen complained. "What's the number for dial-a-whole-church?"

"HEY, YOU GOT DUAL HAND GRIPS!!"

Two holy men walked up and down the same path holding signs that read, "The end is near!" At lunchtime, they sat down together to share some water and dry bread.

The first holy man said, "Something is different today. Everyone who sees my sign looks at me and says 'Duh!'"

"I noticed that too," said the second holy man. "Maybe this afternoon we should try walking on the beach instead of this pier."

A priest, a rabbi, a minister, and a known gambler met once a week for a secret poker game. One poker night, there was a loud knock at the door and a voice said, "Police! Open up!" They hid the cards and the money and opened the door.

The policeman said, "There's been a report of an illegal poker game being held here. Have you been gambling?"

"Of course not," said the priest, "I'm a priest."

"I would never gamble," said the minister. "I'm a minister."

"Not me," said the rabbi. "I'm a rabbi."

Finally it came to the known gambler. The cop asked him, "Have you been gambling?"

The gambler just smiled and said, "With who?"

Are you 45 and getting nowhere? Why not consider the Christian ministry?

Reverend Mel's mom knew he would become a preacher when she heard him say while playing checkers, "Hearken unto their voice, and make them a king."

Bulletin Bloopers

Low self-esteem support group will meet
Thursday at 7:00 p.m. Please use the back door.

Mrs. Roberts will be serving salad without
dressing at this afternoon's potluck lunch.

Helpers are needed! Please sign up on the volunteer sheep.

Latecomers are asked to wait until the service is over to be seated.

"HE'S THE RING BEAR."

Father Matt was conducting the final pre-marriage class for a group of engaged couples. He went around the room and asked each couple if they were prepared to be married. Most of them just said "yes," but Marcia and Ted decided to go into details.

"I think so," said Marcia. "I've got a $5000 wedding dress, ten bridesmaids, a hall that seats 500, the top local caterer, and the absolute best DJ in town."

Father Matt was clearly upset and stammered, "I mean, are you ready spiritually?"

"Calm down, Father, of course we are," said Ted. "We're having ten kinds of fine wine, single malt Scotch, and a keg of micro-brewed beer."

The store manager watched as little Wally wrote something with a crayon on a candy bar and then put it in his pocket. He immediately grabbed the boy and made him empty his pockets. There was the candy bar with the word "Truth" written in crayon across the label.

"Where did you learn how to shoplift like this?" the manager asked him.

"The preacher said it was okay as long as I wrote that word on it," Wally sniffled. "He said, 'The truth shall make you free.'"

Billy was using his father's drill on his new copy of the Good Book. He said it was because he got a Bible, but what he wanted was the holey scriptures.

***

"My baseball coach would want Abraham on his team," baseball expert Art told his friends, "because he obeyed the sign to sacrifice."

NURSERY AND OUTREACH COORDINATOR
BORN
BORN AGAIN
JONNY HAWKINS

An atheist is lost deep in the woods. As he stumbles around in the gathering darkness, he hears some rustling up ahead. He crawls quietly behind a bush and peers through the branches. There in a clearing he sees Bigfoot.

He can't believe what he's seeing and says to himself, "God, I wish there was some way I could record this."

He feels a tap on his shoulder, and there's God standing behind him with a video camera. "I thought you didn't believe in me," God says as he hands the atheist the camera.

The man nods his head. "Up until now, I didn't believe in Bigfoot either."

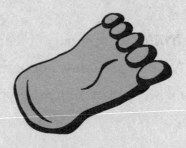

During the absence of our pastor, we enjoyed the rare privilege of hearing a good sermon when Reverend Tom Kelly supplied our pulpit.

Pictures from the seminary picnic are now available. Anyone thinking about becoming a priest should see Father Bill, who will share his negatives.

Our pastor says, "You can call me Doc. I'm your holy plastic surgeon, and I'm here to give you a faith lift."

Little Pat watched a minister wash his hands in a public restroom. "He's not a man of the cloth," he told his dad. "He used the hand dryer."

"I DON'T KNOW ABOUT THE HONEY,
BUT THE MILK MUST COME
FROM HOLY COWS."

The mourners were gathered at the funeral of a Wall Street banker. As the minister eulogized the man's life, he mentioned that the investment banker had once been a millionaire but died without a nickel to his name.

One of those in attendance said, "It's too bad he didn't have more time."

The person sitting behind him leaned over and said, "That sounds like perfect timing to me."

Two cops sat in their car watching a man carry a large statue of Jesus down the street. At every driveway he would stop, put down the statue, and throw a newspaper. Then he picked up the statue, walked down the street to the next driveway, and repeated the process. The cops finally decided this was suspicious enough to check it out. They turned on the flashers and pulled up behind him just as he tossed another newspaper.

When they asked what exactly he was doing, he gave them a simple explanation. "Last week I prayed to Jesus for help to expand my newspaper delivery business, and the next day I found a coupon for free walking shoes. I'm just showing him why what I really need is a truck."

Tina was having a little difficulty with her prayer: "Give us this day our deli bread! Glory be to the Father and to the Son and to the Whole East Coast."

***

Trying to convince his mom he should get an allowance every day instead of once a week, Tommy told his mom, "Jesus wants me to get an allowance every day. That's why the Lord's Prayer says 'Give us this day our daily bread.'"

"LET ME GUESS ... A MINOR
PROPHET?"

Tommy asked if he could send his dad's boss a copy of the Old Testament. When asked why, Tommy replied, "Because he told my dad they weren't going to have any prophets this year."

At income tax time, remember what the Bible says: Beware of false profits!

Bulletin Bloopers

The agenda was adopted...the minutes were approved...the financial secretary gave a grief report.

Please join us as we show our support for Josh and Bridget in preparing for the girth of their child.

We have enough prizes for the games, but we still need some volunteers to run the barbecue for the church carnivore.

The fall Council Retreat will be hell September 20 and 21.

"I'M FROM NEW YORK. I WAS
HOPING TO GET BUFFALO WINGS."

Bob and Jim were standing in line to enter Heaven's First Annual Talent Show. "What's your talent?" Bob asked Jim.

"I can juggle four running chainsaws," said Jim.

"That's impressive," said Bob. "When did you learn you could do that?"

Jim replied, "Five minutes ago when I tried to juggle five of them."

***

Talent show next Saturday night. All interested please sign up after today's services. No talent required.

Pete was quietly praying alone in church when he suddenly heard a voice.

"Pete," the voice said. "This is God. You've lived a long and spiritual life. I've decided to give you a gift for your faithfulness. What would you like?"

Pete thought for a minute and said, "I'd like to have all the money in the world piled up high in my backyard."

"That seems kind of greedy coming from someone like you," God told him.

"You're right," said Pete. "It is greedy and that's not like me. How about this? I've been married for fifty years and I've never been able to understand my wife. For my gift, I'd like to understand her just once."

God replied, "Are tens and twenties okay?"

Diana and Dan request your presents at their wedding.

When asked what he had learned in Sunday school, Jeremy replied, "Adam and Eve were created from an apple tree."

"DEAR GOD, IT'S BILLY...OH, THAT'S RIGHT.
YOU HAVE CALLER ID."

Dear God,

I have a question about something we learned in Sunday School. Were the epistles the wives of the apostles?

Jessica, age 8

Dear God,

If you give me a genie lamp like Aladdin, I will give you anything you want, except my money or my chess set.

Raphael, age 9

The pastor's wife asked little Linda if she had a boyfriend. Linda replied, "Nope. I'm like Jesus—I love them all."

***

Robbie drew a picture of Abraham carrying a lightbulb. He told his teacher, "It's for the sacrificial lamp."

"Eve must have been a really bad musician," said Kenny to his dad. "That's why God told her about the forbidden flute."

***

"My dad is like Jacob," Kelly told her friends. "He did the laundry while Mom was sick, and now I have a coat of many colors."

"I RECOMMEND LOSING A FEW POUNDS
AND DROPPING A COUPLE NOTCHES ON
YOUR BIBLE BELT."

50

Derek and Hugh were lifting weights and admiring their muscles in the mirrors that covered the walls of the gym. Getting philosophical for a moment, Derek posed a question: "Hey, Hugh! Who do you think was the first gym rat in history?"

"My money is on Adam," Hugh replied. "And what he worked on the most was his six-pack abs."

"Why not his arms and legs?" asked Derek.

"He had to work on his abs to distract Eve," Hugh explained. "Otherwise, Eve might notice he was missing a few more ribs."

Deacon Steve always tried to look on the bright side. He said, "Pastor, I have some good news for you! Your biggest critic left the church. But the bad news is, he's been appointed your Head Bishop."

***

Reverend Jerome will discuss the health risks of obesity, and then the choir will sing, "There's a Wideness in God's Mercy."

You could tell Father Jim was happy with his sermon because he ended by saying, "Many have yawned, but few are dozin'."

***

Everyone knew what Reverend Joe's favorite sport was when he commented, "If I were a betting man, I'd take Daniel over the lions by 10."

When asked to explain his job, the minister said, "The Lord is the Great Physician, and I'm His HMO."

Phyllis Green would like to thank all of you who assisted her after her fall at last week's services. We are happy to report that the doctors X-rated her arms and legs and found no fractures.

Al, the chronic complainer, passed away after a long life and found himself in heaven. Not surprisingly, he had nothing but complaints. "The feathers on these wings make me sneeze," Al told St. Peter. St. Peter said there was nothing he could do about this.

Al had another complaint. "Those harpists! Don't they know any rock songs?" St. Peter said he couldn't do anything about that either.

Al wouldn't give up. "And my room is in between two baseball fans who are constantly arguing about the Padres and the Cardinals!" St. Peter said it was out of his control.

Al was furious. "If you don't do something about these things, I'm going to sue!"

St. Peter just laughed and replied, "Good luck finding a lawyer up here."

Dear God,

Instead of letting people die and having to make new ones, why don't you just keep the ones you already have?

Kathy, age 8

At an atheist funeral: "Here lies an atheist, all dressed up and nowhere to go."

Noah rang the bell of the ark and his three sons came running. "Grab some buckets and start bailing water!" he yelled to Shem and Ham. "Japheth! You take this wood and hammer and nails, jump into the water, swim under the ark, and patch the holes!"

As Japheth went over the side of the ark, Shem asked Ham, "Why did dad give Japheth such a hard job?"

Ham replied, "Because Japheth is the one who convinced him to bring two termites."

Words from the Pulpit

Father Joe tried to appeal to the baby boomers in church when he said, "Some of you on the stairway to heaven need to start praying for an elevator."

At the service before Halloween, Pastor Martha told the congregation not to put their faith in false gourds.

"CPR classes will be held in the church hall next Saturday," the deacon announced. "And now let us close by singing: 'Lord, Send a Revival.'"

"Father Hans is the pastor of our mission parish in Bavaria," said Father Vic. "I like to think of him as our German Shepherd."

"WHEN IT COMES TO PAYING THE WAGES OF SIN ... IS THERE A GRACE PERIOD?"

I want to remind the choir and all special sinners to be at the park by 4:30 PM for warmup and sound checks.

Jason scolded his dad, who was helping a neighbor paint his house. He told him: "The commandment says 'Thou shalt not cover thy neighbor's house!'"

Will didn't want his family to be under stress when he died, so he decided to get a prepaid funeral. The funeral director went through a long checklist, and Will picked out his casket, his flowers, the hymns to play, and even the make of the hearse to ride in.

Finally the director got to the last question and quietly asked Will, "Are there any words you'd like for me to say on that day?"

Will thought for a minute and said, "Yeah. 'Call 911—I think he's breathing again!'"

The funeral for the late basketball coach was well attended, with former players filling the pews and current players acting as tall-bearers.

Please place your donation in the envelope along with the deceased person you want remembered.

"WOULD YOU LIKE ME
TO SAY REGULAR GRACE
OR AMAZING GRACE?"

Emily's mother asked her what they were supposed to do before each meal. Emily replied, "We braise the Lord and thank him for the food."

After the Ladies' Association potluck dinner, we will take a moment to pray for the sick.

Jack was in a minor car accident and went to the emergency room to get checked out. Everything seemed fine, but he still had a pain in his side so the doctor prescribed a painkiller. Jack took one of the pills before bed and fell asleep with the pain in his side still bothering him.

In his dream, he was visited by God. Jack thought it was the end. "No!" he pleaded. "I'm too young to die!"

"Relax," God told him. "I'm just here to tell you that your pain is from your rib and it needs to be taken out."

"No!" Jack pleaded. "I'm too old to marry another woman!"

Oscar must have been thinking about eating lunch when he asked his Sunday school teacher if Adam and Eve had a choice between original sin or extra crispy.

***

One of the first things Adam and Eve did after leaving Eden was raise Cain.

"I WAS EXCOMMUNICATED
FROM SUNDAY SCHOOL!"

Please note that a three-year-old teacher is needed for Sunday school. Experience preferred.

Dear God,

We read that Thomas Edison made light. But in Sunday school, we learned that you did it. I bet he stole your idea.

Michael, age 9

Bulletin Bloopers

For anyone donating adult gifts, see the church secretary.

Let us give thanks to Susan Lewis for donating an organ to our music department.

Next Saturday we will hold our semiannual
Personal Growth Workshop. For parents,
complimentary day care will be provided at a
cost of $5 per child.

The blessing of the pets will be held this Sunday.
Bowls, collars, and leashes will be sold for a
small flea.

"HE'S A TV EVANGELIST."

Father Jeremy keeps up with all the latest diet crazes, including low-carb. He lets parishioners opt to say: "Give us this day our daily meat."

***

The football-loving minister caught the coin he flipped and said to the congregation, "You've won the toss and elected to receive the Holy Spirit!"

A grandmother read Bible stories to her grandson, Paul. She read, "The man named Lot was warned to take his wife and flee out of the city, but his wife looked back and turned to salt."

Paul asked, "What happened to the flea?"

***

The Scrabble game was interrupted when Junior swallowed an X. "Mom! I think we need to perform an X-orcism," Mary yelled.

"I know why Moses parted the Red Sea," Jill informed the class. "He was wearing a white robe and didn't want it to get any red stains."

"I can always pick out the occasional churchgoers at Christmas time just by listening to them," said Reverend Jill.

"I wish I could do that," said Reverend Vicki. "What's your secret?"

"It's easy," explained Reverend Jill. "I go to the mall. The occasional churchgoers are the ones whose prayer requests are the same as their list for Santa."

Seen on Signs

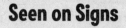

THE MORNING SERMON:
WOMEN IN THE CHURCH

THE EVENING SERMON:
RISE UP, O MEN OF GOD

**On a battered
church sign:**

SINNERS
REPAINT!

To welcome a new church pastor:

PLEASE WELCOME
PASTOR DONNA,
A CARING INDIVIDUAL
WHO LOVES
HURTING PEOPLE.

Matt wrote down all the things he wanted to do before the end of the world. He called it his "apoca-list."

***

After listening to relatives talk at her great-aunt's funeral, Sondra made a list of all the things she owned and whom they should go to if she died, then taped a piece of gum to the bottom. She said it was her "last will and peppermint."

Chuck's young friends were teasing him about going to vacation Bible school while they played baseball instead. "I'll bet you're just going there to read all the stories about S-E-X we heard about that are in the Bible," one of them told him.

"No one says anything about S-E-X in the Bible we use," Chuck told them. "It's the King James Virgin."

After listening to his older sister talk on her cell phone for hours, Tyler started calling the nearby cellular phone tower the Tower of Babble.

Jerry thought he'd impress his grandson by telling him stories about when he used to attend tent revival meetings. "One night I saw something that was truly miraculous," he told his grandson. "A man was filled with the spirit and began speaking in tongues."

"I see that every day, Grandpa," the boy said. "At the deli. First the butcher speaks in tongues, then he speaks in lunch meats, then he asks mom to make up her mind already."

"Do you think my friend Mary Catherine goes to a different church every week?" Missy asked her mom. "She told me she was a roaming Catholic."

A young man went to a Baptist preacher to discuss joining his church. "I have some concerns," the young man told the minister. "I've heard your church has some pretty strict rules about sex."

"Nonsense!" said the minister. "We have no rules about it. You can do it any way you want. Well, except standing up."

"Why not standing up?" the young man asked.

The minister whispered, "Then it would be dancing."

As several churchgoers got up to prepare for a buffet lunch, our minister announced, "The ladies leaving the sanctuary will have some hot buns for us after the service."

***

Reverend Alex blessed the all-natural cereal being served at the vegetarian prayer breakfast, then told the attendants: "And now, let us be filled with the holy groats."

Every shopper in church woke up when the preacher yelled during his sermon: "And the Wal-Marts of Jericho came tumbling down!"

Our pastor is a real comedian. He calls the Ten Commandments "God's Top Ten Signs You May Not Be Going to Heaven."

"WHAT YOU SAID ABOUT HEAVEN WAS INTERESTING. I'M GONNA SEE IF IT CHECKS OUT WITH OPRAH."

Chuck, an expensive Wall Street lawyer, dies and goes to heaven. When he arrives, he's surprised to be greeted by tens of thousands of people cheering and holding signs that read, "Welcome to heaven, Chuck!" Angels lift him up and fly him over the crowd so he can see that the crowd numbers in the millions, all cheering for him.

The angels place Chuck down gently in front of St. Peter, who shakes his hand and pats him on the back. Chuck puffs up his chest and brags, "I guess you don't get too many big-time Wall Street lawyers up here."

"They're not cheering because you're a lawyer," says St. Peter. "It's because you lived to be 137 years old. That's a new record."

"I'm not 137. I'm only 50," says Chuck.

St. Peter pulls out a report and says, "Not according to your billable hours."

Two old gents were taking a nice slow walk along the beach. Every few feet, one of them would bend down, pick up an oyster, and whisper "I'm sorry." He'd put it back down, walk a few feet, pick up another oyster, whisper "I'm sorry," and put it back down.

This went on a few more times and the other gent was starting to get worried. "Have you lost your marbles or is this some kind of new exercise program?" he asked his friend.

"Neither," the other replied. "I figure I'm going to be in heaven one day and I don't want to feel guilty when I walk up to the Pearly Gate."

The man had led a terrible life and done a lot of terrible things—committing crimes, acting like a jerk, swearing. Yet, when he died, he was surprised to find himself in heaven talking to St. Peter.

"I can't believe the streets of heaven are paved with gold!" he told St. Peter.

"That's why you're here," Peter told him. "We had a bad winter and the plows tore up the streets. We've got one really big hole to fill. That's where you come in, Chuck."

"YOUR SERMON HIT CLOSE TO HOME ...
IT WAS PERFECT FOR MY
NEXT-DOOR NEIGHBOR."

Dear Pastor,

Are there any devils on earth? I think there may be one in my class.

Carla, age 8

Dear God,

If we come back as something, please don't let me come back as Donna, because I hate her.

Dennis, age 5

"I hope you saved your receipts," Quentin told the groom before the wedding. "My dad said you have to exchange your vows."

***

Father Ben hated when marriage ceremonies were interrupted by picture-taking, so he told the congregation: "Even if your spirit is willing, let your flash be weak."

Malcolm, the ring bearer, walked up to the minister as he was preparing for the marriage service and asked why he wasn't wearing his bulletproof vest. "You need to be careful," he told him. "My dad said this was going to be a shotgun wedding."

"SERIOUSLY? IT'S SIN-RESISTANT?"

For Sale: Suits, pants, dresses!

VINTAGE CLOTHING SALE
THIS SATURDAY IN THE
CHURCH BASEMENT.
STOP BY AND CHECK OUT
THE SATAN DRESSES.

Bulletin Bloopers

Please sign up to attend the Prayer and Fasting Conference. The cost of attending includes meals.

John and Susan have been lifelong friends. This marriage marks the end of that friendship.

Tuesday at 4:00 PM, we will be serving homemade ice cream. All ladies giving milk please come early.

***

Bilingual chicken dinner this Sunday at noon.

THE CHICKEN

EL POLLO

"ATTENDANCE IS DROPPING BECAUSE
YOUR BLOG SITE IS SO POPULAR."

A note to the pastor from the church secretary during his absence:

Good news: The Women's Guild voted to send you a get-well card. Bad news: The vote passed 31-30.

For God so loved the world that He did not send a committee.

After listening to a sermon about heaven, the rich old billionaire went home and picked up his Bible for the first time in many years. He spent hours and hours in his den, reading it slowly and carefully, page by page.

His wife was shocked and pleased. "I've never seen you read the Good Book like that before," she said. "Are you looking for a particular passage?"

"No," he told her. "I'm looking for an address. If I can't take my money with me, maybe I can ship it ahead of time."

Bob and Gary were discussing what they wanted their family to put in the casket at their funerals. "I want to be holding a Bible and a rose," said Bob.

"Not me," said Gary. "I want to be holding a pack of needles. That way, when I meet a rich guy in heaven, I can make him show me the camel trick."

There's no bigger boxing fan than Father O'Conner. He always calls his favorite book about hell "Don King's Inferno."

The parking lot has been repainted. We're asking all children in the parish to help their parents stay inside the lines.

Little Wayne could always be found sitting under the Christmas tree singing his favorite song: "A Wayne in the Manger."

Ray carefully folded a paper airplane and put it next to the figure on the top of the Christmas tree. "He's a Blue Angel," he explained.

Nick was competitive in everything he did. While the other kids were content to make snow angels, he would hold a toy sword in one hand and make snow archangels.

"MAY I HAVE A WORD?..."

During the marriage ceremony poor little Meredith was seated next to a guest who was in need of some deodorant. Meredith wrinkled her nose and said, "Pee-yew! You should have gone to the wedding shower!"

The shoppers at the kitchen supply store laughed as Scott marched around carrying a utensil holder while singing loudly: "A mighty fork rest is our God."

Everyone is excited about the upcoming wedding of Brad and Melody. They are having a "country style" wedding, and everyone is invited to join them as they exchange cows in the church courtyard.

The windows in the church have been replaced with bulletproof glass. It is now ready for weddings again.

✳✳✳

The bride nearly fainted when Reverend Hal asked, "Do you, Robert, take Melinda to be your awful wedded wife?"

"WOW! TALK ABOUT FAMILY VALUES!"

It was Oscar's first day on the job at the Christian bookstore and he wanted to make a good impression. His boss told him to pack 100 Bibles in a box and take them to the package delivery store.

Oscar came back an hour later with a big smile on his face, holding a page torn from each of the Bibles. When the boss asked what they were, Oscar beamed and bragged, "I saved you a bunch of money. The man at the shipping store said it would cost extra if the box contained anything breakable, so I took out the Ten Commandments!"

Three atheists and a Christian were playing golf and arguing about the existence of God. "I'm going to prove to you that God exists," the Christian told the atheists. "I'm going to put on this blindfold and pray to God to help me sink this 60-foot putt."

The Christian golfer donned the blindfold, bowed his head in prayer, stood over where he thought the ball was, and swung his putter. He hit the ball and it miraculously rolled across the green and into the hole.

"That's just luck," one atheist said.

From up above, a loud voice said, "He's right."

The Christian golfer pointed to heaven and shouted, "Do you need more proof?"

The atheist replied, "Yes, it's still three against two."

"There were giants on the earth in those days," the preacher read from Genesis.

From the back, a voice asked, "San Francisco or New York?"

Gerry hit Father Dave with a theological baseball question. "Who does God root for when the Padres play the Angels?"

The inventor of the final exam died and was pleased to find himself standing at the Pearly Gates. However, he became puzzled when St. Peter led him in and walked him past every priest, rabbi, and minister up there to a fantastic apartment in the best neighborhood in heaven.

"I'm just the humble inventor of the final exam," he told St. Peter. "What have I done to deserve a place so much nicer than theirs?"

"It's simple," said St. Peter. "You're responsible for getting more people to pray than any holy man in history."

Bulletin Bloopers

We are looking for new members for our Community Stewardship Group. Next Saturday at 11:00 AM, we will meet at Will Rogers Park to eat and collect garbage.

***

A bean supper will be held prior to our Church Mission meeting. Music will follow.

Part-time secretary needed to answer church phone and give massages to the pastor.

***

Bertha Belch, a missionary from Africa, will be speaking tonight at Calvary Methodist. Come hear Bertha Belch all the way from Africa.

Signs of God's Presence?

SIGN ON THE DAIRY CASE AT A CHRISTIAN GROCERY STORE:

I AM MY BUTTER'S KEEPER.

SIGN ON A FRUIT STAND RUN BY MONKS:

AMAZING GRAPES

SIGN ON A WASHROOM
AT CHURCH:

AMEN'S
ROOM

SIGN ON A TRUCK
FOR A REHAB COMPANY:

REPAINT,
AND THIN
NO MORE!

A trio called The Resurrection was scheduled to sing at a church revival, but a storm postponed their performance.

The pastor changed the sign outside to read:

THE RESURRECTION HAS BEEN POSTPONED

The Sunday school teacher asked her class if anyone could recite the tenth commandment. Susie raised her hand, stood tall, and said, "Thou shalt not take the covers off thy neighbor's wife."

"God was the first police officer," said Nancy, "because on the seventh day he arrested."

"Who discovered what many believe are the original writings of the Bible?" asked the teacher.

Donna raised her hand and said, "The Dead Sea Trolls?"

***

In answer to a question in his Bible studies class, Bob wrote: "When the Israelites left, the Egyptians tried to catch them racing through the dessert."

"ARE BUTTERFLIES LITTLE REMINDERS
THAT THERE ARE ANGELS AMONG US?"